HOWARD BRENTON

Howard Brenton was born in Portsmouth in 1942. ...   /s
include *Christie in Love* (Portable Theatre, 1969); *Revenge* (Theatre
Upstairs, 1969); *Magnificence* (Royal Court Theatre, 1973); *The
Churchill Play* (Nottingham Playhouse, 1974, and twice revived by
the RSC, 1978 and 1988); *Bloody Poetry* (Foco Novo, 1984, and
Royal Court Theatre, 1987); *Weapons of Happiness* (National
Theatre, Evening Standard Award, 1976); *Epsom Downs* (Joint Stock
Theatre, 1977); *Sore Throats* (RSC, 1978); *The Romans in Britain*
(National Theatre, 1980, revived at the Crucible Theatre, Sheffield,
2006); *Thirteenth Night* (RSC, 1981); *The Genius* (1983), *Greenland*
(1988) and *Berlin Bertie* (1992), all presented by the Royal Court;
Kit's Play (RADA Jerwood Theatre, 2000); *Paul* (National Theatre,
2005); *In Extremis* (Shakespeare's Globe, 2006 and 2007); *Never So
Good* (National Theatre, 2008); *The Ragged Trousered
Philanthropists* adapted from the novel by Robert Tressell (Liverpool
Everyman and Chichester Festival Theatre, 2010); *Anne Boleyn*
(Shakespeare's Globe, 2010 and 2011); *55 Days* (Hampstead
Theatre, 2012); *#aiww: The Arrest of Ai Weiwei* (Hampstead Theatre,
2013); *The Guffin* (NT Connections, 2013); *Drawing the Line*
(Hampstead Theatre, 2013); *Doctor Scroggy's War* (Shakespeare's
Globe, 2014); *Lawrence After Arabia* (Hampstead Theatre, 2016);
The Blinding Light (Jermyn Street Theatre, 2017) and *The Shadow
Factory* (Nuffield Theatre, Southampton, 2018 and 2019).

Collaborations with other writers include *Brassneck* (with David
Hare, Nottingham Playhouse, 1972); *Pravda* (with David Hare,
National Theatre, Evening Standard Award, 1985) and *Moscow
Gold* (with Tariq Ali, RSC, 1990).

Versions of classics include *The Life of Galileo* (1980) and *Danton's
Death* (1982) both for the National Theatre, Goethe's *Faust*
(1995/6) for the RSC, a new version of *Danton's Death* for the
National Theatre (2010), *Dances of Death* (2013) for the Gate
Theatre, *Miss Julie* (2017 and 2019) and *Creditors* (2019), both for
Jermyn Street Theatre and Theatre by the Lake, Keswick.

He wrote thirteen episodes of the BBC1 drama series *Spooks*
(2001–05, BAFTA Best Drama Series, 2003).

Howard Brenton

JUDE

NICK HERN BOOKS
London
www.nickhernbooks.co.uk

A Nick Hern Book

Jude first published in Great Britain as a paperback original in 2019 by Nick Hern Books Limited, The Glasshouse, 49a Goldhawk Road, London W12 8QP

Howard Brenton has asserted his right to be identified as the author of this work

Cover image: photography by Shaun Webb

Designed and typeset by Nick Hern Books, London
Printed in the UK by Mimeo Ltd, Huntingdon, Cambridgeshire PE29 6XX

A CIP catalogue record for this book is available from the British Library

ISBN 978 1 84842 859 1

Jude was first performed at Hampstead Theatre, London, on 26 April 2019, with the following cast:

EURIPIDES/ROGER SYLVESTER   Paul Brennen
MARK NASRANI/BOB CHALLOW   Merch Hüsey
DEIDRE CASS   Caroline Loncq
JACK DONN   Luke MacGregor
JUDITH NASRANI   Isabella Nefar
PAT NASH   Shanaya Rafaat
MARTHA NASRANI   Anna Savva
SALLY PHILLOTSON   Emily Taaffe

Director   Edward Hall
Designer   Ashley Martin-Davis
Lighting   Peter Mumford
Sound   John Leonard
Composer   Simon Slater
Casting   Susie Parriss CDG

In memory of Howard Davies

Characters

JUDITH NASRANI
MARTHA NASRANI, *her aunt*
JACK DONN, *her lover*
MARK NASRANI, *her cousin*
SALLY PHILLOTSON, *a teacher*
BOB CHALLOW, *a pigman*
DEIDRE CASS, *an Oxford Professor*
PAT NASH
ROGER SYLVESTER
EURIPIDES

*Euripides to double as Roger Sylvester, Mark Nasrani to double
as Bob Challow*

Setting

Act One: At Waterlooville

Act Two: At Oxford, later again at Waterlooville

*This text went to press before the end of rehearsals and so may
differ slightly from the play as performed.*

ACT ONE: At Waterlooville

Scene One

SALLY PHILLOTSON *has discovered* JUDITH NASRANI *stealing a book.* JUDITH *hides it behind her back.*

SALLY. What's that?

JUDITH. What's what?

SALLY. A book?

JUDITH. So?

SALLY. Oh for Godsake, if you want to – read something, ask and you can borrow it.

JUDITH. No I want to steal it.

SALLY. I'm sorry?

JUDITH. Stealing makes it better.

SALLY. Makes what better?

JUDITH. The book.

SALLY. Why?

    JUDITH *shrugs.*

JUDITH. More tasty.

    And grins.

SALLY. Look, if we're going to understand each other – I mean your first day, I'd hoped – oh, give it to me.

    With a sudden movement, JUDITH *throws the book to her. Startled,* SALLY *catches it awkwardly. She looks at it.*

    Euripides? In Greek?

    JUDITH *shrugs, a movement of her right hand. It gives a contemptuous impression.*

What was the idea, flog it on eBay? Well I don't know what you'd have got for it, it's not exactly a Marvel-comic shocker – though I s'pose, in its day, *Medea* – but – you were going to, what? Pilfer your way through my flat, then flit away, never to be seen again? You've really let me down, Judith.

JUDITH. It's a disease.

SALLY. Petty thieving, a medical problem? I s'pose that's some kind of sociological excuse –

JUDITH. Reading. It's sick. That's what my aunt says.

SALLY. What does this aunt do?

JUDITH *with a shrug.*

JUDITH. Works at the Payless.

SALLY. And she doesn't like you reading? I mean you can re– sorry –

JUDITH. Fuck off.

SALLY. Yes, that was – of me –

But JUDITH *rushes at* SALLY, *who flinches.* JUDITH *grabs the book, turns away and opens it. She reads – carefully – the first line of* Medea.

JUDITH. Εἴθ' ὤφελ' Ἀργοῦς μὴ διαπτάσθαι σκάφος

SALLY *is stunned.*

But JUDITH *begins to struggle with a translation.*

How I – want – no, wanted, no – wished? Wished – the *Argo* – *Argo*! Jason's ship, sexy beast, wan't he – μὴ διαπτάσθαι, what's that?

SALLY. Verb –

JUDITH. Yeah I know it's a verb –

SALLY. To fly through. Past tense. And it's negative. Can be about a journey.

JUDITH *stares at the line, speaking it to herself. Then –*

JUDITH. How – I wish – the *Argo* – had never – reached – the land.

A pause.

SALLY. All right. Was it your school, back in Syria? What, an elite, a party school?

JUDITH *is looking at her in her shutdown mode.*

I mean how did you learn Greek?

JUDITH. Church.

SALLY. Church?

JUDITH. My aunt goes to church. They have a jumble sale.

SALLY. But – aren't you, I assumed – aren't you Muslim?

JUDITH. You tell me.

SALLY. No, I mean –

JUDITH. I'm what you think I am, in't I.

SALLY. And you think I think you're – (*Stops herself.*) I don't want this to get complicated. I just want my flat cleaned.

JUDITH *shrugs.*

So, jumble sale?

JUDITH. Yeah.

SALLY. And you – found Ancient Greek there.

JUDITH. There was this 'Teach Yourself' book. And an oinky old dictionary.

SALLY. Oinky?

JUDITH (*shrug*). Covers all buggered.

SALLY. And you bought them?

JUDITH, *nothing.*

Of course not.

JUDITH *in her shutdown-and-stare mode.*

A pause.

Did someone at the college put you up to this?

JUDITH. Up to the Greek?

SALLY. It's Colin, isn't it, bloody Colin. God keep us from men who are practical jokers – I mean I know he wants classical studies off the curriculum but – get me to go into a staff meeting and say 'Little refugee girl stole my Euripides, I have found a genius?' – Egg all over my face. So own up. That it? Mr Chalmers at Southsea College, he got you to fake knowing Greek?

JUDITH. Are you like – saying I'm faking?

SALLY. I mean – I'm asking –

JUDITH. Right! Fake! It's all fake! The Greeks knew that, wake, fake, yeah even being awake, that's fake! That's what they say – don't wake up, it'll kill you! So fuck your stupid job and fuck you!

She slams the book down on the ground, kicks the cleaning equipment over and is leaving. But suddenly she turns on SALLY *and shouts at her.*

μῆνιν ἄειδε θεὰ Πηληϊάδεω Ἀχιλῆος

JUDITH *exits.*

And –

Scene Two

SALLY *and* PAT NASH.

SALLY. Can I smoke?

PAT. Not really.

A pause.

So, she shouted at you and left. And –

SALLY. I was – shocked.

PAT. Cos little foreign cleaners aren't meant to know Ancient Greek.

SALLY. No. Yes. No.

PAT. What was it she shouted?

SALLY. The first line of the *Iliad*.

PAT. Which is?

SALLY. Obviously the police don't read Homer.

PAT. No need, we see enough blood poured in the sand.

SALLY. 'Sing Goddess of the rage of Achilles.'

PAT considers her for a moment.

PAT. What do you think she meant?

SALLY. 'Sing Goddess of the rage of Judith Nasrani'? Look, that young woman has ruined enough of my life –

PAT. Really? I thought you ruined hers.

SALLY. Excuse me?

PAT. At Oxford?

SALLY. I tried to stop what happened. Wanted to stop it.

A pause.

'Blood poured in the sand.' You do know Homer.

A pause.

Why have I been brought here? Hotel room? I – I mean what
is this?

PAT. You know what it is. You played with fire and now it's
playing with you.

SALLY. I'm not staying here to be –

A pause.

I mean you've not cautioned, arrested me or – maybe you
can't. If you're –

A pause.

SIS have no powers of arrest, if that's what you are?

PAT, *still as a stone.*

So I'm walking out of here, now.

She does not move.

A pause.

Poisoned cloak.

PAT. I'm sorry?

SALLY. I think I'm going to –

She is near to retching.

Oh God, what has she done?

PAT. Do you want some water?

SALLY. Stiff G and T more like.

PAT. We'll have a drink, girls together, after.

SALLY. What, after I've betrayed her?

PAT. Let me give you some advice, Sally. Think of yourself.
What *you* hold dear, what *you* hold to be true. You know this
is serious. That's why it's scaring you shitless.

SALLY. In God's name, tell me what she's done!

PAT. We just need to find her. (*A beat.*) Okay recap, four years ago, you're teaching in Waterlooville, just outside Portsmouth, you need a cleaner.

SALLY. I – was finishing an MA and with teaching at the college – well, busy life, things get into a tip.

PAT. Don't they. MA about what?

SALLY. Pericles.

PAT. Oh him.

SALLY. Yes him.

PAT. The doomed champion of Athenian democracy.

SALLY. You have done Classics. Where?

PAT. Let's just say up a dead end.

SALLY. You're Oxbridge, aren't you.

PAT. Am I?

SALLY. We have to hide it these days, don't we. The curse of belonging to a dying elite.

PAT laughs.

PAT. Sounds like fun. But no, that's not where I belong. Not at all.

Her face sets after the laughter.

A pause.

So. You needed your flat cleaned but you didn't ring a cleaning agency.

SALLY. No.

PAT. You had a charitable feeling.

SALLY. Well, yes –

PAT. And you saw this girl's name on the board at the Refugee Centre.

SALLY. Yes!

PAT. Went there a lot, did you?

A pause.

The Centre. A group met there. Something called a 'Resistance Workshop'?

SALLY. That was – an informal thing.

PAT. Informally resisting what?

SALLY. People like you.

PAT *sighs.*

PAT. Don't go smart-arse with me, Sally.

SALLY. It was just a – women's resource group. Trying to help immigrants with problems.

PAT. You know the council closed the Centre.

SALLY. I left Waterlooville –

PAT. Closed it because of information received from the security forces.

SALLY. Look, understand, I don't do that stuff any more.

PAT. Stuff?

SALLY. Getting involved! Activism. Caring about the bloody world.

PAT. But you did care about Judith. And very much got involved.

SALLY. It –

A pause.

It was the line she translated, on the spot. It was perfect. 'How I wished the *Argo* had never reached the land.' You know how difficult Ancient Greek is – to teach it to yourself? Horrible.

PAT. So you convinced yourself on the spot, she was some kind of genius?

SALLY. Not meant to believe in 'genius', are we. If someone's gifted, they've got a class advantage – household of books, foreign holidays, music. Or it's medical – you know, Mozart? Aspergic, wasn't he. Nothing's from nature, it's all nurture. You think you're bright, special, blessed with a gift? Your mummy and daddy went to Oxbridge – count your privilege. Any of us can sing, write, act, do maths, paint the Sistine Chapel, it's just society, capitalism, the patriarchy that's fucking me up, stopping me from being – Euripides, Virginia Woolf. Not me, not dull me, encased in this – genetic prison, called myself, this mould of mediocrity. So any tall poppies that grow on our democratic anthill – cut them down. All the bright flowers have got to be phoney. Nurture not nature, I did believe that. Then this – this –

PAT. Little foreigner?

SALLY. This slip of a girl from nowhere nicks a book and –

She stops.

PAT. And – the world turned inside out?

SALLY. I told her she she – had a kink o' some kind in her, in her head, just to stop her. Stop the –

She hesitates.

PAT. Stop the what?

SALLY. The vision. It wasn't just her freakish ability with language. She – saw through to behind the words. It was like she had a direct line to – I was going to say to 'the gods'.

PAT. That's handy.

SALLY. I know, it sounds stupid.

PAT. Not at all. We deal with people with a direct line to God all the time.

A pause.

So. So you saw her name on a board at the Waterlooville Refugee Centre, you thought you'd do some good, hire a girl who needed the money to clean your flat. You had a row, then –

SALLY. Then –

PAT *exits,* SALLY *still on the stage.*

Scene Three

Allotment.

MARTHA NASRANI. *She has a garden fork. A wheelbarrow is beside her.*

SALLY. Mrs Nasrani?

MARTHA. Who says so?

SALLY. Well, at the shop, they said you'd be out here.

MARTHA. So, here I am. Out here.

SALLY. My name is Sally Phillotson. You're Judith's aunt?

A pause.

MARTHA. I don't know a Judith.

SALLY. At the Payless, they said –

MARTHA. There is no Judith.

SALLY. But you are Martha Nasrani and this is your allotment?

MARTHA. If you won't leave me alone then let me be rude.
    Please bugger off, yes?

SALLY reels.

SALLY. I think we've got off on the wrong foot –

MARTHA. What do I care about your foot? I know who you are!
    The National Allotment Society have given me the right. So
    tell those Waterlooville gardeners they can send all their
    lawyers but this is my plot. I keep it very well, look, no stupid
    sunflowers. Why grow sunflowers when you can eat leeks?

SALLY. Actually you could dry sunflower seeds, they're full of
    vitamin Bs – no. Look – I'm nothing to do with allotments.
    I do some voluntary work at the Refugee Centre, your
    niece's name was –

MARTHA. I have nothing to do with that place!

SALLY. But –

MARTHA. There are bad people there.

SALLY. Actually it's just a little charity trying –

MARTHA. It is an organisation! It will be corrupt. They all are, parties, charities. I know. From what happened to my family.

SALLY. There are good-hearted people –

MARTHA. Oh yes. But for every good heart there is a snooper. Is that what you are, a snooper?

SALLY. No –

MARTHA. From immigration?

SALLY. This is simply about – look, I gave your niece a cleaning job. We – had a misunderstanding. I want to put things right. You do know that Judith is a very gifted young woman?

JACK DONN is entering. He carries a bunch of flowers.

MARTHA. For the very last time I have no niece!

JACK. Judith about?

MARTHA turns on him.

Mrs Nasrani, pleased to meet you. I'm Jack Donn. I'm a – I know Judith.

MARTHA. There is no Judith!

He laughs.

JACK. Yeah! Look I sort of want to see you.

MARTHA. Well I do not want to see you.

JACK. You don't understand.

MARTHA. Oh I understand young men like you.

JACK. No, really, I want to do the old-world thing, like I know you people like to do things right.

MARTHA. 'You people'? What kind of people is that?

She lifts the fork.

JACK. I want to talk to you about your niece Judith!

MARTHA. I do not have a niece called Judith, and if I did have a niece called Judith, I would not have you sniffing around her! Go away, young man, or I will do serious gardening on you!

JACK. Yeah? You and whose army, fucking Syria's?

SALLY. I think you'd better go.

JACK. I got a business. I'm in meat.

MARTHA. I don't care what you're in.

JACK. I just want to do the old-world thing!

SALLY. Well you have and now you can go.

A pause.

The flowers.

JACK. These were for you. I love her, y'know. I can look after her and I will. And there in't nothing you can fucking do about it!

SALLY. Really I –

But he throws the flowers down and exits.

MARTHA. The dogs, out there in the night, at the fences. You spend every drop, awake all night, to keep them out. Then, in broad daylight, they come.

She sighs.

SALLY *wants to comfort her but cannot bring herself to do so.*

I don't have the money.

SALLY. Money?

MARTHA. To pay for what she broke.

SALLY. Nothing was broken. Well, maybe a few of my assumptions!

She tries to laugh. MARTHA *stares.*

Mrs Nasrani, I think your niece has a very precious gift.

MARTHA. The girl is a lump.

SALLY. She's brilliant at languages.

MARTHA. She has turned into an English lump. She moons around, like all the English girls, they moon around.

SALLY. She's teaching herself Greek –

MARTHA. I tell you she is lumpy, clumsy, a clumsy dreamer, just like her father.

SALLY. Her father – is he –

A beat. That stare from MARTHA *– aggressive, defensive.*

MARTHA. He is in heaven. Perhaps.

SALLY. Oh I'm so very sorry –

MARTHA. Did she lose her temper?

SALLY. Well –

MARTHA. Just like her mother.

SALLY. And her mother –

MARTHA. For my sins I am all the family that God has left her. Did she steal from you?

SALLY. It was just a book –

MARTHA. Always, books! She went to Portsmouth, to the public library, to steal. Books in Latin, a language she can't speak! There's something – (*Gesture.*) wound up loose in that lump's head. It's shaming. I throw the books away when I find them, in other people's wheelie bins.

SALLY. I'm a teacher, a teacher at South Hants College. I'm a classicist.

MARTHA. Is that good?

SALLY. Good? Well – yes! I teach a module – a course – on Greek and Latin. Actually it's called Ancient Paradigms of Western Imperialism – but it's Greek and Latin. And I'd like to teach Judith.

A pause.

MARTHA. She can't go to your college, she passed no exams.

SALLY. But didn't her teachers notice?

MARTHA. She was never there. Now could you go, my leeks cry out to me.

SALLY. Just bear with me – she's left school? She's over sixteen?

MARTHA *stares*.

Well she's over sixteen or she's not.

MARTHA. Not. Or – not really.

SALLY. So she's under sixteen.

MARTHA. Over or otherwise, fifteen, fourteen, it depends who's asking.

SALLY. You lie about her age? You're worried about her leave to remain?

MARTHA *clams up*.

So you told the authorities she was younger than she really was, when she came?

MARTHA, *still clammed up*.

She got to England alone, that it? You were her only family and took her in? But when she's eighteen she'll have to apply for leave to remain and –

MARTHA. You are a snooper!

SALLY. No!

MARTHA. An informer! We knew all about informers in Tadmur.

SALLY. Tadmur? That's – Palmyra. You're from Palmyra?

MARTHA, *distressed*.

MARTHA. I am always saying, I have always said and say again and again, I am grateful to English people, grateful to

England, grateful to your Government, I will never say
anything else. Now, please –

A gesture from her deep fatigue – 'go away'.

SALLY. I don't mean to distress you – I simply want to teach
your niece.

MARTHA. I have no money to pay.

SALLY. No, teach her for free. Maybe you don't realise, she
could – go to university. Education is a wonderful thing.

MARTHA *scoffs*.

MARTHA. In Syria we were all educated. What good has it
done us?

A beat.

The temples of Palmyra were beautiful in the morning. They
had a rose colour.

SALLY. I know, I got there, in my gap – yes. In the morning.

MARTHA. Then the heathens blew them up.

SALLY. And that's when you left?

A beat.

MARTHA. Before.

SALLY. I'm sorry I don't mean to pry, I'd – just like to know.

MARTHA. Why?

SALLY. Well – maybe I can help.

MARTHA. I expect you are a kind woman, a well-meaning
woman, Miss –

SALLY. Phillotson, Sally –

MARTHA. But my life is calm now. I have work in the shop,
I have this plot. And all I want is calm. Thank you.

SALLY. But it's such a waste.

MARTHA *laughs*.

MARTHA. A waste. A waste. Good morning, Miss Phillotson.

They turn away from each other. But then –

Then the heathens blew it up. Teach the girl if you can. But pay her to clean, get her to clean with all your friends. All I care is she earns her keep.

SALLY. That's wonderful. Ask her to come round this evening, about six. Your niece could do great things, Ms Nasrani.

MARTHA. All I ask is don't betray her. Our family have had enough of betrayal.

Scene Four

Bare stage.

JUDITH (*off*). Yeah yeah yeah, c'mon, Jack! Jack Jack Jack! Yeah!

A half-drunk bottle of vodka bounces then rolls onto the stage.

Then JUDITH and JACK roll onto the stage, laughing. His trousers are round his ankles, her skirt is up, they are covered in hay. They come to rest in each other's arms, she lying across him.

Well, that's it in the straw!

JACK. Fucking prickles and all.

JUDITH. I love the prickles!

JACK. But it was my bum getting 'em.

JUDITH. Pleasure 'n' pain, in't it.

JACK. That's what it is, thanks for explaining that. How d'you always end up on top anyway?

JUDITH. It's à la mode.

JACK. 'À la' what?

JUDITH. Trending.

JACK. Oh great, yeah. May really trend one of these days, give you a proper seeing-to.

JUDITH. Oooh ooh, wow! Where's this seeing-to gonna happen then?

JACK. Well –

JUDITH. I mean in what? We've done sand, Hayling Island, done the sea there too, and wet grass, that field up at The Bat and Ball – remember the starlings?

JACK. God, doll, you were – off the scale –

JUDITH. Weren't I just, what else –

JACK. Don't forget the cabbage patch –

JUDITH. My aunt's allotment.

JACK. Bit of a nasty stalk experience.

JUDITH. So where's it going to be? This final once-in-a-life-time-seeing-to fuck?

JACK. Well there's always the mud at my place. Always fancied a muddy shag.

JUDITH. Fancy on, lover. Where's the vodka?

JACK. You sort of – chucked it away at a big moment. Like you do.

JUDITH. What, chuck things away at big moments, do I?

JACK. Yeah, like when you – you know.

JUDITH. What? What? What you trying to say?

She tickles.

JACK. Nah nah I love it, I really do, vodka, vodka, over there –

JUDITH. Oh yeah.

She stands pushing down her clothes, retrieves the bottle.

He pulls up his pants and trousers.

She swigs from the bottle. Gives it to JACK, *who swigs.*

JACK. Judy, I did something.

JUDITH. What?

JACK. I went to see your aunt.

A pause.

JUDITH. Why you do that?

He hesitates, shifty.

JACK. Anyway, I went to see her.

JUDITH. But why?

JACK. I wanted to ask her – about us getting married.

A pause.

JUDITH. Us what?

JACK. I wanted to do the old-worldy thing.

JUDITH. The old-worldy thing –

JACK. Get in a positive light with her. By doing the right thing.

JUDITH. You asked my aunt if I could marry you?

JACK. I've looked into it. She's your guardian, right? Nearest of kin? Need her permission, don't we. I mean, sixteen in't you.

JUDITH. Am I? (*A beat.*) Anyway, in't 'the right thing' to ask me first?

JACK. Well! Yeah. But.

JUDITH. But what?

JACK. But we sort of know, don't we.

JUDITH. Do we?

JACK. I mean the sex being so great.

JUDITH. What's the sex got to do with it?

JACK. Oh c'mon! You and me, we're naturals.

JUDITH. Naturals for what?

JACK. Stuff.

JUDITH. Stuff.

JACK. Life. Together.

JUDITH. Oh that 'stuff'.

A pause.

What did my aunt say, then?

JACK. I – didn't get the words out right.

JUDITH. You don't with her.

JACK. She made me feel stupid.

JUDITH. Join the club.

JACK. Well sod her. We'll do it anyway.

JUDITH. Yeah? Little thing, lover, you still han't actually
asked me.

JACK. Oh. No. Right. (*A beat.*) Well, here. Will you marry me?

JUDITH. No fucking way.

A silence.

JACK. Yeah!

Laughs.

JUDITH. I won't.

JACK. Nah.

JUDITH. What do you mean 'nah'?

JACK. Nah you're saying yes.

JUDITH. Don't let's do yes-no, yes-no.

JACK. But we're right into each other, in't we!

JUDITH. We just fuck like rabbits.

JACK. Right, so let's get married.

JUDITH. I don't want to be Mr and Mrs Bunny.

JACK. But I'll save you.

JUDITH. Save me?

JACK. They won't chuck you out. British national's wife. I mean they're getting really heavy about you lot.

JUDITH. My lot?

JACK. All you fucking Arabs 'n' Africans.

JUDITH *laughing*.

JUDITH. What a charmer is my lover!

JACK. Judy, I googled your status.

JUDITH. Ooh! Kinky! Google me up in leather 'n' chains –

JACK. Be serious about this! For fucksake, when you're eighteen you'll need permanent permission to stay.

JUDITH. I'll get asylum.

JACK. No way. You bunked off school, you're working illegally.

JUDITH. I'm not working.

JACK. The cleaning –

JUDITH. That's just on the side –

JACK. Jesus, for someone so bright you're so bloody stupid! No way will you get asylum.

JUDITH. I will.

JACK. You won't.

JUDITH. Will, won't, yes, no – you don't know my story!

JACK. Only cos you won't tell it me.

JUDITH. That's cos it's mine!

JACK. What, you think I won't understand?

JUDITH. You won't. You really – will not.

JACK. Just try me.

A pause.

JUDITH. 'Oh sacred rivers, flow backward to your sources
That the great order of the world may be reversed.'

A pause.

JACK. Greek bollocks?

JUDITH. It's a prayer.

JACK, *angry in his incomprehension. Clenches his first, hits at the air. Calms down.*

A pause.

JACK. Okay okay! I don't know how you got into the country and I don't care. What's fucking Syria to me, one more foreign toilet. All that matters is – You're just – here. Like out o' nowhere. Cos I love you, Judy.

A pause.

JUDITH. I want to go to Oxford.

JACK. Oxford?

JUDITH. Yeah, why not?

JACK. Well – house prices are a choker for a start. And it's an 'orrible town, all lattes and weird craft beers. Then there's fucking students everywhere, toffy noses stuck up their arses. Nah, stupid living there.

JUDITH. I don't want to live there, I want to be a student.

JACK. Student? You? Why?

JUDITH. So I can get a toffy nose to stick up my arse.

JACK. Yeah, sexy!

And JUDITH *is in her clammed-up mode.*

You're not serious.

Nothing from her.

How could – (*Laughs.*) like, I know you eat books for breakfast – but, I mean, Oxford fucking University?

JUDITH. I'm going to get a degree.

JACK. Studying what? Vodka-bottle chucking?

JUDITH. The classics.

JACK. Classics? What – old Jaguars? Or the horses, yeah, go study with the punters, Oxford William Hills, get a degree spot-betting on Cheltenham!

JUDITH. Take me serious, Jack. I warn you, you don't take me serious, I'll scratch your eyes out.

A pause.

JACK. 'Classics.' You mean the bollocks, don't you.

JUDITH. Yeah, the bollocks.

JACK. Okay, I'll be serious.

He walks up and down, getting his attack together, then turns on her.

Oxford University? You'll need A levels up to your armpits. And you han't even got GCSEs cos of bunking off school. How you going to get A levels in Greek?

JUDITH. And Latin. And Classical Civilisation. That's all you need. Three As.

JACK. Yeah but Oxford's all 'yah yahs' and load's o' cash, upper-class twit-fucks and Chelsea cunts in floaty dresses. You'll never get into that.

JUDITH. I will, I'll wow the dons.

JACK. Dons?

JUDITH. The old men who run the place. I'll tick their boxes all over. They'll cream 'emselves over me – little asylum seeker. Speaking Greek.

JACK. Judy, this – fantasy. I mean you're not even at school!

JUDITH. I've got a teacher.

JACK. Yeah? Who?

JUDITH. A woman with Euripides.

JACK. Sounds like a disease.

JUDITH. It is. No cure.

A beat.

JACK. You are taking the piss –

JUDITH. I'm not –

JACK. Royally taking the piss!

JUDITH. I am going to go to Oxford University. I will get a first-class degree, in Classics, Greats, which is what they call it, Greats, great things, wonderful things. A first – and I will change my life!

They look at other, breathing.

'Nother vodka?

JACK. Well.

A beat.

I s'pose – anything that's on offer. Like me.

JUDITH. On offer, are you? Special offer?

JACK. Buy anything and get me free.

JUDITH. So sweet. Come here.

They embrace.

JUDITH *leaves,* JACK *stays on the stage.*

Scene Five

JACK *and* ROGER SYLVESTER.

ROGER. I'm not the FSA.

> *A moment.*

> *Then* JACK *bolts.* ROGER *rugby-tackles him. They fall to the ground.* ROGER *expertly pinions him.*

JACK. My meat's good!

ROGER. Mr Donn, calm down –

JACK. There's nothing wrong with my meat!

ROGER. Calm down and we can have a conversation –

JACK. The council don't bother, why's the FSA coming all over me of a sudden?

ROGER. I am not the Food Standards Agency.

JACK. I'm busting a gut to make a living here! That's all!

ROGER. Last time – this is not about your pig meat, which I'm sure is daisy fresh and succulent, though you may illegally slaughter the odd stolen animal. Now, stand up and we will try to be fucking civil, right?

> ROGER *lets* JACK *go, who stands.*

> You've got a son.

JACK. Timmy? This is about Timmy? What, I been rugger-tackled by the Social Services? Fuck, what's wrong? It the other kids at the child-minder? They pick on him cos he's so bright – why are kids so cruel? And I thought Demarra was good, lots of local mums and dads use her – where is he now, don't say he's in A 'n' E, I better –

ROGER. This isn't about Timothy, it's about his mother.

> *A pause.*

JACK. The cunt's come out of the woodwork, has she?

ROGER. A way of putting it.

JACK. Four years, and fuck-all. Absolutely zilch. Not a text, not a call, not a postcard. Now out of nowhere, this crap! Well she's not getting Timmy! I'll fight all the way, take to the woods. My son is with me.

ROGER. So your relationship with your wife is – tense?

JACK, *taken aback.*

JACK. Yeah! Well – yeah! Took off, didn't she. Nicked all the cash in the house too.

ROGER. Just to be clear, that was four years ago, and you have heard nothing from her, at all?

JACK. I said – she took off!

ROGER. Did she ever talk about a cousin, called Mark?

A pause.

JACK. What are you? Not the social, not some kind of lawyer. CID? But you don't feel like the wuzzy wuzzy.

ROGER. I'm just a man who's here to ask you a very serious question, Jack. Which is this. If Judith was in trouble, deep trouble, would you help her?

JACK. What kind of deep trouble?

ROGER. Deep.

A beat.

JACK. Get off my property.

ROGER. No no no –

JACK. I'm not talking to you.

ROGER. Still love her?

JACK. Off!

ROGER. You talk about her being your wife, but, here's a thing, searching the Registry of Marriages, I could not find any record of you actually tying the knot.

JACK. Well. We was going to but her aunt – next of kin –

ROGER. Well that's a real bummer, Jack. Judith's permission to stay can be revoked, any time. And, when we find her, it almost certainly will be. Along with other things that may happen to her – and – since you are not married, her son's presence in the country could also well be – in danger.

JACK. Timmy's four years old! You'd send a four-year-old, born here, with an English dad – what, back to Syria?

ROGER. The days of zero tolerance are drawing in. But Jack, we can help. Get Timmy's status sorted. We'll let the Immigration Services know you're an upright citizen. Onside. Which you are, aren't you, as an 'English Dad'? Well and truly onside?

A pause.

JACK. I swear to you I do not know where she is. What else can I do? What am I, fucking powerless here?

ROGER. Just – tell me about what you remember about your break-up.

JACK. How will that help?

ROGER. Memory's like a game of poker, there's always a tell.

A beat.

JACK. I've got to pick up Timmy from the child-minder in half an hour –

ROGER. Someone's doing that.

JACK. Who?

ROGER. Don't worry, she'll say you're busy and she's a friend.

JACK. But how do you know the address –

A pause.

You're all over us, aren't you.

ROGER. Fortress Britain? Needs be, Jack.

JACK. Judith's in real kind of shit, in't she.

ROGER. Just tell me about the break-up.

JACK. It – it started with that teacher she got thick with.

ROGER. You mean Sally Phillotson?

JACK. Yeah. That's the cow.

Scene Six

SALLY*'s flat.*

SALLY. *Enter* JUDITH *with a notebook.*

JUDITH. Sal! Hi! Listen!

Flipping over pages of the notebook – copious writing.

In the *Iliad*. All the similes. Describing war, fighting, death – they're all from peace. Home. Nature. Listen!

As she reads SALLY *becomes increasingly irritated.*

'So the cries of the Greeks urged on their war-lust
Thick-and-fast as the snows that fall on a winter day.'

'The battle line held as when a woman, weaving, holds
The balance of the weight and the wool on the loom.'

'As the East and South winds clash in violent squalls
Deep in a mountain valley and oak and ash
Whip their long sharp branches against each other
So Achaeans and Trojans clashed and hacked each other.'

SALLY. Yes but –

JUDITH *ignores her.*

JUDITH. 'As a working widow holds the scale
And lifts the weight and the wool together
Balancing one against the other

Struggling to win a living for her children –
So powerful armies drew dead even battle lines.'

SALLY. Yes but –

JUDITH. And here's a great one about builders –

'...the ranks pulled closer
As a stone mason packs stones in a wall
Granite block on granite block, so the crested helmets
The war shields, massed tight, man against man.'

SALLY. Yes but –

JUDITH. And there are streams, storms, and baking bread, and
animals in the forests, and threshing floors, the things of
everyday life, all as – swords slashed, shields banged into
bodies. Over and over and over.

Fired up, JUDITH *stops.*

SALLY. It's a convention.

JUDITH. No, it means something.

SALLY. It's a trick, a – rhetorical device.

JUDITH. Yeah yeah, it's spoken, chanted, sung to an audience,
Homer's using pictures, everyday life, what his listeners
knew from around them, but – it's got a message.

SALLY. You're making the mistake of thinking there really was
someone called Homer. There wasn't. The poem's come out of
countless repetitions, changes, in – village squares, in private
houses, in city squares, elaborating a story everyone knew.

JUDITH. No no! Homer was real. It's one voice.

SALLY. Saying what? War is bad? Isn't that – just crass?

JUDITH. He's more than *saying.* And it's – *more* than a message.

SALLY. So it's what?

A pause.

JUDITH. The music.

SALLY. Music.

JUDITH. Of the horror. (*A beat.*) Killings told with pictures of peace. Over and over, till you can't bear it. And it's horrible and it's beautiful, all at the same time.

A moment.

After all, it's a god singing, in't it. Through him.

SALLY. So. Where did you get all this?

JUDITH. Get it?

SALLY. Well it's not your idea. There have been lots of studies on Homeric similes.

JUDITH. Yeah yeah, the Harvard Homer Project, that crap.

SALLY. The Harvard Project is hardly crap –

JUDITH. Yeah it is! Cos they don't ask what the similes *mean*? But I got the answer – got it from nowhere – from me –

SALLY. Judith, if you're going to write exam essays, you must acknowledge sources.

JUDITH. But I'm the source –

SALLY. Plagiarism is the great academic sin.

JUDITH. You think I nicked it! Sal, I didn't, I swear. I read Homer, that's what I hear.

SALLY. Oh God –

JUDITH. It's from me! In me! I hear him. Please, please –

SALLY. All right, all right, I believe you. (*Low.*) What's it matter anyway?

JUDITH. Sorry?

SALLY. I've been offered a postgraduate research post at Christminster College, Oxford. They're being really wonderful. I can finish my DPhil.

JUDITH. That's great, Sal! We got to celebrate –

SALLY. So I'm leaving.

JUDITH. For Oxford? Hey, like – I'll come too. Lots of cleaning there – colleges, big houses of big clever people, I bet – and you can carry on teaching me. And I'll get my A levels, and you'll get me into your college, and we'll do great things together!

SALLY. Judith, you've got a baby.

JUDITH. So?

SALLY. The problems, childcare – and – well, your domestic situation.

JUDITH. What you mean?

SALLY. Your husband's meat thing.

JUDITH. 'Meat thing.'

SALLY. If you're involved with what he does, and I s'pose you're bound to be, the police –

JUDITH. Why you all down on me, of a sudden?

SALLY. I can't teach you any more.

A pause.

Please understand. This is a really big thing for me.

JUDITH. But why can't you teach me?

SALLY. I will have some first-year students but –

JUDITH. So I'll join in!

SALLY. The college won't like me teaching outside. I'll only be teaching undergraduates.

JUDITH. Well I'll pretend to be one, go about drinking pints of warm beer –

SALLY. Judith, I've helped you all I can.

JUDITH. What about my A levels?

SALLY. You've got a great gift, be happy with that.

JUDITH. You're abandoning me!

SALLY. Look, I've got you a present, the Jebb edition of
Sophocles –

JUDITH. Fuck Sophocles! Man sleeps with his mother? Crude
stuff. Euripides is the one. We go wild you know.

SALLY. Who do?

JUDITH. Pets. Cats, dogs, thrown out, pets like me, we go furry
– what's the word –

SALLY. Feral –

JUDITH. Feral – get diseases on the street, bite –

SALLY. Judith, don't –

JUDITH. I've been your pet!

SALLY. That's – so deeply – unfair!

JUDITH. When Jason dumped Medea, remember what she did
to his wife.

SALLY *laughs*.

SALLY. What, you're going to wrap me up in a poison cloak?

JUDITH. Yeah! Great! One day you'll find it all around you.
Tighter and tighter.

SALLY. You think you're clever, and you are, in a way, with the
languages. But it's just a kink. In your head.

JUDITH. Think I'm a freak, do you?

SALLY. I think you're a little bitch on the make. Maybe that's
how you –

Stops.

JUDITH. How I what? Oh! You mean that's how I got into your
country? By being a bitch?

During SALLY*'s next speech* JUDITH *is set in stone.*

SALLY. No I didn't mean, no – but you never talked about how
you got out of Syria. (*A beat.*) The journey. (*A beat.*) Who
you were with. What happened. (*A beat.*) Turkey? Greece,
Albania, then, what, across to Italy? France, Germany?
Calais? (*A beat.*) What you had to do. I mean I can only
begin to – (*A beat.*) I mean I can't. (*A beat.*) Were you
always on your own? (*A beat.*) Or – did you lose your family
on the way, or –

A long silence.

Oh, for fucksake, I –

JUDITH. You came to me, Sally. You said I had a gift. You said
you'd help me.

SALLY. I have helped you.

JUDITH. So be grateful and piss off?

SALLY. Yes! I'm sorry! It's my life!

JUDITH. Dodge down.

SALLY. What?

JUDITH. Through a hole. In the wire.

SALLY. I don't –

JUDITH *runs off.*

Oh sod sod sod.

Scene Seven

Night. It's cold. Enter JUDITH. *She has a vodka bottle and is drinking.*

JUDITH. Don't wake up, it'll kill you.

She drinks.

And in the dark, as chorus, the single figure of EURIPIDES *appears, masked.*

Acty – acty – Miss Activist. Acty acty libby liberal – pet, was I? Showed me off to your friends – oh meet my geni-weenius, little refuguee-ey – she cleans my toilet and does Greek –

EURIPIDES. Sally's done everything for you –

JUDITH. It's me that done everything for me –
            And it's not about me

Not about her

It's about 'it' –

          The 'thing'
          The Greek –

EURIPIDES. But it gets personal
          When the people you're trying to help
             are –

JUDITH. Are what, deeply fucking unhelpful?

EURIPIDES. It's the simple thing so hard to do
          To help

All you can do is a pin-prick
          Pin in the flesh of a brute of a world
But if enough prick the beast
          In the end he'll die

The great monster astride the world
          Wounded by a billion cuts
Will crawl into the forest
          Then we'll set the trees alight

And history will burn
                    And we'll begin again
Green shoots in the ashes
                    A new world

Free, held in common
                    With no borders

JUDITH. No borders!

EURIPIDES. Meanwhile
                    Being radical in Hampshire
Is a pain in the bum

JUDITH. And they need their fucking flats cleaned

EURIPIDES. They need their fucking flats cleaned

JUDITH. I really thought Sally was nice and wanted to help.

EURIPIDES *fading*.

EURIPIDES. Artemis rescued you
                    She deceived their eyes
Stole you away from danger
                    Through the azure sky
Set you down
                    In this strange land

EURIPIDES *has gone*.

JUDITH. Artemis, yes –
                    What's the bitch
Got in store for me?

She drinks deep.

It begins to snow.

Lights of a vehicle across the stage. It draws up. Stops. Doors opening, one slammed. The voices off of BOB CHALLOW *and* JACK.

JACK (*off*). I'll get the bolt gun.

BOB. No, do that in the shed, her bowels'll go. Let's get on with it, I don't want her messing up my van –

JACK (*off*). Back up through the gate. I'll get the yard light on.

JACK *runs on. He switches on a powerful yard light, a strong shaft of light across the stage.*

He sees JUDITH.

What you doing out here?

JUDITH (*slurred*). I'm discussing liberals, good people, trouble is they got their heads up their arses –

Stares at her for a moment.

JACK. You are totally ratted!

JUDITH. S'deliberate –

JACK. Is with you, in't it –

JUDITH. S'a holy state, Dionysius –

JACK. You knew we were getting the pig tonight!

JUDITH. Little piggy –

JACK. Where's Timmy?

JUDITH. In the house.

JACK. You left him –

JUDITH. He's fine, little man, dribbly dribbly –

JACK. You know this is a big night for me, get back in, sober up!

BOB *enters (played by the later* MARK *actor).*

BOB. Jack – oh hello, Judy.

JUDITH. Hello, Bob, you're English, smelly up there, is it, but kind o' comfy?

BOB. Up where?

JUDITH. Your arse.

BOB. She's ratted.

JUDITH. I am.

JACK. Judy, in the house –

BOB. I'm not doing this with your missus in that state.

JUDITH. I'm not his missus.

JACK. Not for asking!

JUDITH. Wants to be the master, don't you, master piggy man!

BOB (*mutter*). Jesus, never shag foreign cunt –

JUDITH. What you say, what you say?

JACK. Judy, shut up, this is business! Bob, the deal was –

BOB. Fuck the deal, I'm off.

JACK. You said you'd tell me how to do this –

BOB. Yeah but you said she was up to help.

JUDITH. Are the men in trouble?

BOB. I told you, fiddling records to nick meat out the back of the abattoir is one thing –

JACK. Back of the abattoir where you work –

BOB. – but stealing live animals, it's a different fucking order o' reality!

JACK. I'm expanding. I got these two freezers off that bloke at Hambling. And that gave me the idea and hey, I mean – you saw tonight, it's dead easy. No security on the farm. On any of 'em. If we'd had a lorry we could have had two more finishers, easy.

JUDITH (*waving the bottle at him*). S'the great piggy rustler.

JACK. Bob, for me.

A moment.

BOB. I'll get her in the shed then I'm off.

JACK. The two of us can't do it!

BOB. You'll have to.

JUDITH. Stick the pig! I'll stick the pig!

A blackout.

Scene Eight

Lights up slowly. Next morning. Pristine snow.

JUDITH *staggers on, carrying a pail.*

JUDITH. Did that, did I? How she squealed. Rage then despair.
Then the bolt gun. And her innards went. It was – beautiful.
And there she is, hung, draining – dripping – this –

*She puts the pail down. She dips her arm in and pulls it out
covered in blood.*

Quis hic locus, quae regio, quae mundi plaga?

*She lifts her arm out of the pail, covered in blood. She begins
to drip it over the snow.*

What is this place, this region, this area of the world?

She drips spirals of blood.

I was great with the languages, Daddy. All the way to the
Hungarian border, my little sweet-talker, you said. That
Albanian with the phones. Got us through the wire. In the
snow. But I couldn't do the Hungarian, not like Greek, Latin,
ugly sounds, clacky tins banged, I couldn't do the language,
couldn't stop the men – cruel men – in the snow – you – in
the snow.

*She throws the pail of blood across the snow/stage. She
crumples, holds her face in the hands.*

Enter JACK.

JACK. Tim wants his breakfast, I could do with a fry-up an'
all –

He stops at the sight of her.

What the fuck you doing?

JUDITH. You can talk wire away, you know.

JACK. That blood's for black pudding!

JUDITH. You can get through.

JACK. Black pudding – bit of fun – the vindaloo of sausages, blokes go ape for it – flog it in the pubs –

JUDITH. Apes? Vindaloo sausages? I don't – are you Hungarian?

JACK. Judy, come inside, clean up –

She scuttles back, away from him.

JUDITH. But I learnt enough words in a day, didn't I. Kérem, ne bántson. Kérem ne bántson. Please don't hurt me.

JACK. I don't want to hurt you, Judy. Why do you think that?

He helps her stand. But then she pulls away.

JUDITH. I've got to get through. The wire, the border. To Oxford. It's like a garden there. Behind old walls. And they talk English. And Latin. And Greek.

JACK. Yeah. Yeah, course.

JUDITH. I'm going now.

JACK. Yeah.

For a moment they are still.

JUDITH. I mean it!

She pulls away and is about to run.

JACK. Oh f–

A blackout.

End of Act One.

ACT TWO: At Oxford then again at Waterlooville

Scene One

Requiem sounds: a bell tolls, a choir sings.

Then enter SALLY *and* DEIDRE CASS, *a professor. They are in appropriate ceremonial gowns.*

DEIDRE. Did you know Philip Bletchley?

SALLY. Way above my cloud level. What was he like?

DEIDRE. Not a man to meet in the rose garden.

SALLY. Ah.

DEIDRE. At least a college chapel requiem gives you the chance to get the trappings out.

She laughs and flicks her gown.

SALLY. The trappings that trap us.

DEIDRE. Personally I find a kind of comfort in the flummery of ritual.

SALLY. It's drained of meaning.

DEIDRE. Absolutely. But now and then, in these ideological times, it's a relief not to have to mean anything. Walk with me?

SALLY. Love to.

DEIDRE. Mind if I vape?

SALLY. No, please.

They walk, DEIDRE *starting up a vaping device.*

They exit as – a distance away – JUDITH *enters with* MARK.

JUDITH. Look, through the arch –

MARK. Judith, this isn't good –

JUDITH. No, look! The lawn, the quad, people in gowns, like crows with fur on their wings. They've been having a ceremony –

MARK. What are we doing here?

JUDITH. It's Christminster College!

MARK. It's just old walls with CCTV cameras.

JUDITH. It's heaven on earth!

MARK. Don't make light of heaven, it's blasphemous.

JUDITH *laughs. She is in high spirits.*

'The most hideous voice is the braying of the ass.'

JUDITH. Sorry?

MARK. What the Koran says about taking things in vain.

JUDITH. My dreamy, spirity cousin! Working in that shop's real bad for you! Religious books leaking some kind of gas – religion gas –

MARK. Stop it.

JUDITH. 'Inter Faith Resource and Café' – how can Christians and Muslims be 'Inter'? If Muhammad was God's messenger, then Jesus and his Gospels are fake news, big time.

MARK. Be careful of what's in your mouth.

JUDITH. Yeah, tongues, tricky things, got a life of their own – lalalalala! Speaking in tongues. Goobledi-gobbledi, God's a woman! Ooh! Naughty tongue.

MARK. You're so – adolescent.

JUDITH. Adolescent! Oooh! Adolescence, from the Latin, adulescens, 'growing, young', present participle of adolescere, 'ripen' – is that me? Am I ripening?

MARK. Ripe? No, just mad.

JUDITH. See how they stand, like in a frieze, on a temple.

A pause.

MARK. Let's go home. The cameras – they're looking at us.

Enter SALLY *and* DEIDRE, *as if coming out of the college.*

JUDITH *sees them and pulls* MARK *back.*

JUDITH. No, wait!

DEIDRE. Sally, sweetheart, I've been meaning to ask you – will you be my indexer?

SALLY. But isn't your publisher –

DEIDRE. They're being fucking awful about it. Gerald wants to give it to some in-house little bumboy of his. I mean twenty years working on the bloody thing, life's work, la la et cetera, I need someone I trust. And that is not my editor's catamite.

SALLY. Yes, I mean, of course –

DEIDRE. I know the college has given you a teaching load beyond the call, needs must in these dog days. But there'd be a pittance.

SALLY. Deidre, I'd love to do it.

She wouldn't.

DEIDRE. An interesting-looking young woman is staring at us.

SALLY. Oh no, please not, world –

DEIDRE. Know her?

JUDITH. It's bloody Sally –

MARK. Oh, the one –

JUDITH. Yeah, the bitch who let me down. But I'm going to forgive her. C'mon –

JUDITH grabs his hand, as if she is looking for a gap in traffic to cross the street. MARK *pulls his hand away.*

MARK. No, they're university heathens.

JUDITH. But you sell books to them!

MARK. Yeah, I wash them off me every day. I'm getting the bus.

JUDITH stamps her foot.

JUDITH. Mark! Mark!

He exits.

JUDITH calls out, as if running through the traffic.

Sally, Sally, it's me!

SALLY. Judith. How wonderful. How – how long have you been in Oxford?

JUDITH. Three weeks. I've done my A levels!

SALLY. You went back to school?

JUDITH. Nah, did them on my own. External, Havant College.

SALLY. Right!

DEIDRE. Sally, please explain this young person.

She smiles. JUDITH frowns at her.

SALLY. Deidre, this is – Judith Nasrani. And, Judith, this is Deidre Cass.

DEIDRE. Hi, Judith.

JUDITH. Deidre Cass? Professor of Classical Language and Literature at Christminster?

DEIDRE. I blush.

JUDITH. I read your book on Dionysius.

DEIDRE. The blush is beetroot.

SALLY. Judith's –

DEIDRE. So – you live at home, or –

JUDITH. I'm a cleaner.

DEIDRE. Dear God, a working-class reader at last? How do you two know each other?

SALLY. I taught Judith at Waterlooville.

DEIDRE. The college –

JUDITH. No, I was cleaning her flat and nicked a book. So she took me up.

DEIDRE. Romantic.

JUDITH. Then she dropped me down.

A big smile at SALLY.

SALLY. It –

DEIDRE. A levels, self-taught? Results out on Monday. What subjects?

JUDITH. Latin, Greek, Classical Civilisation.

DEIDRE. Ambitious.

JUDITH. Not really. It's only languages. They're just like breathing, aren't they? Breath, words, thought, it's just part of – being alive.

DEIDRE *is genuinely taken aback by this.* SALLY *is irritated.*

SALLY. Well it's been nice –

DEIDRE. Where are you from?

JUDITH. Does it matter?

DEIDRE. I suppose not. What did you make of my book?

JUDITH. The chapter on the feminisation of Pentheus went wonky.

DEIDRE. Wonky.

JUDITH. When the god makes the king dress as a Maenad, he is showing him his true nature, not imposing one on him.

DEIDRE. Arguable. But you're imposing a feminist trope on a very ancient text.

JUDITH. But that's what Euripides meant.

DEIDRE. You can't know that.

JUDITH. Yes I can. He told me.

DEIDRE. Really?

An antsy SALLY intervenes.

SALLY. Judith, look, I've got my old email, why don't you –

DEIDRE. Where are you staying?

JUDITH. Out at Rose Hill. I'm kipping with my cousin Mark.

DEIDRE. You mean the pretty boy who ran off? Have I seen him somewhere?

JUDITH. He works in the interfaith bookshop, off the high street. Sexy in't he. He's theologically unstable but I'm working on that. You going to let me in?

DEIDRE. In?

JUDITH. Into Christminster.

A pause.

DEIDRE. Look – Miss Nasrani, yes? Let me know your results. You can leave a message with my secretary at the college. Maybe I can give you some advice.

JUDITH. You mean a place?

SALLY. For Godsake!

JUDITH. I got to go cos of Mark. I'll phone you, Deidre. My results will be brilliant!

She exits, running.

DEIDRE. Goodness me.

SALLY. Absolutely.

DEIDRE. What is she?

SALLY. Syrian.

DEIDRE. So she's Muslim.

SALLY. Actually her background's Christian.

DEIDRE. Exotic.

SALLY. I don't think that's the – appropriate world.

DEIDRE. Naughty me. Still, lovely skin. Any idea of her
immigration status?

SALLY. Murky, to say the least. And there was a child, God
knows where that is. Deidre, you're not seriously thinking –

DEIDRE. No, no. But the college is under terrible diversity
pressure. I weary being told how shocking it is to be white
and bright.

SALLY. I warn you, she's trouble.

DEIDRE. Clingy?

SALLY. When I told her I was coming here and couldn't help
her any more we had a terrible row, she –

DEIDRE. What?

SALLY. Frightened me.

DEIDRE. All the same – female, Arab, from a persecuted
religious minority, a single mum and self-taught – I can hear
the boxes ticking themselves. She won't get good As, will she?

SALLY. No. No. She's in for a big shock. No.

DEIDRE. Well then.

They turn away.

Scene Two

JUDITH lies on a single mattress on the floor, a bed in Tracey Emin-style disorder.

She is asleep. Then she opens her eyes.

Out of the dark appears the masked EURIPIDES.

JUDITH. Daddy, I won't let you down!

EURIPIDES. I saw you and your father in Turkey
                              Konak Square, Izmir
    Little girl selling cigarettes

JUDITH. Stuck in Turkey, all the money gone

EURIPIDES. He told you don't sell cigarettes –

JUDITH. But, Daddy, we need
                              Money to buy lifebelts

EURIPIDES. For Oxford your father weeping
                              To see you trading
    With men in dark alleys

JUDITH. Cheeky kid, that was me
                              flogging cigs

EURIPIDES. For this, across the rolling
                              Waters of the grey sea –

JUDITH. Buy lifebelts for the *Argo*, Daddy –

EURIPIDES. His dream
                              His clever little girl
    At Oxford England

    For Oxford, the sharp snow
                              Sharp wire
    Albanian border

    Sharp sound, a shot

JUDITH. Daddy, Daddy!

EURIPIDES. For Oxford, the kindness of strangers
                              Against the unkind world

Gently prising your fingers
> From your father's neck

JUDITH. Daddy, Daddy, I'm nearly there!

And again she wakes.

Scene Three

JUDITH *reaches for the empty vodka bottle, it rolls away.*

Enter MARK.

MARK. Oh no, not stains again.

JUDITH. Again and again, dear coz.

MARK. This is my floor, you know.

JUDITH. No it's the world's. The low flat floor of the world. I'm sinking in it. Floor of the world.

MARK. The stupid talk of yours –

JUDITH. S'a metaphor – language – thinking – (*Slur.*) metaphorically, it's what makes us conscious.

MARK. You are conscious because you think you're falling through the floor?

JUDITH. S'human.

MARK. Goodnight, Judith.

He turns away.

JUDITH. No no wait! I want to talk.

MARK. Do it in the morning.

JUDITH. I'm cleaning at five.

MARK. Then sleep the booze off.

JUDITH. No alko's just a daemon, the Greeks knew all about daemons, I'll get it out of my head, now!

She scrabbles her hands in her hair, shakes her head vigorously.

Out out out out!

A beat.

There, see him go, orangey leather wings, straight up through the ceiling! And I'm sober.

MARK. I'm tired, Judith –

JUDITH. Please, it's a big day tomorrow.

MARK. Why big?

JUDITH. My A-level results!

MARK. Oh yeah.

JUDITH. You forgot!

MARK. You're not the centre of the world.

JUDITH. No? Oh bother.

She laughs.

MARK. Look, could you –

JUDITH. What?

MARK. Your leg.

JUDITH. Oh.

She covers up and suppresses a giggle.

MARK. You're going to pass anyway, aren't you?

JUDITH. Passing in't enough, I've got to be brilliant.

MARK. Yeah, well.

JUDITH. Well, what?

MARK. Y'know.

JUDITH. I don't, what?

MARK. Going to the university? Don't you see, they'll never let you in.

JUDITH. Why not?

MARK. Cos of who we are.

JUDITH. No, they're scholars, scientists, thinkers, all they believe in is excellence.

MARK. We're trash to them, Judith.

JUDITH. Well thanks for the encouragement. God, sometimes family's like a lead balloon.

She picks up the vodka bottle, upends it, nothing in it.

MARK. Anyway, why do you go for all that Greek stuff? It's heathen, they should knock it all down.

JUDITH. 'Stuff' like – the theatre at Epidaurus? The Acropolis in Athens? Palmyra, Mark? Our home?

MARK. Yeah, yeah! Bulldoze the lot. Wipe out their history.

JUDITH. It's our history, yours, mine, everyone's –

MARK. It's not. It's the Kafirs.

JUDITH. The Ka–

She laughs.

You look so stupid with that word in your mouth.

MARK. No, I don't.

JUDITH. Like you're trying to sit up straighter than you can and pop your eyes out.

He slumps.

MARK. No way!

JUDITH. Where's this crap coming from?

MARK. I read. And go online.

JUDITH. What's going on with you, Mark?

MARK *is shy of this*.

MARK. It's that –

He hesitates.

I'm on a spiritual journey.

JUDITH. Who the fuck isn't?

MARK. Everyone thinks I'm a Muslim.

JUDITH. I know, you don't get a chance to say 'But I'm a Christian, there are Christians in Syria.'

MARK. Yeah, why are people so ignorant in England?

JUDITH. Funny, in't it. I mean my father always said 'In England people are free.' I s'pose he meant free to be pig ignorant.

MARK. I begin to feel 'You think I'm a Muslim, okay I'll be one.'

JUDITH. You're not serious, you can't be.

MARK. I dunno. But it rings true. Like when the Koran says 'Do not walk proudly on the earth.' (*A beat.*) 'Do not walk proudly on the earth.'

JUDITH. But I want to be – proud, walking on the earth.

MARK. Well that's just you. Actually, they say everyone in the world is a Muslim, but won't acknowledge it. We're all followers of the Prophet. We just – don't know it.

She considers for a moment.

JUDITH. Yeah. All of us simply needing a message to wake us up to what we really are. Wish that was true.

He won't look at her.

MARK. I –

JUDITH. What?

MARK. No.

JUDITH. What? What? Oh you could bloody drive me mad.

MARK. It's not something a man should say.

JUDITH. Just say it anyway.

MARK. I believe there must be beauty in the world.

He is mortified. JUDITH, *very gently.*

JUDITH. Why isn't that – manly?

He shrugs.

MARK. It's corny, it's stupid.

JUDITH. Mark, I read a lot, Greek poetry, Latin poetry, in Greek, in Latin! Homer, Sappho, Virgil, Horace, Ovid – and I tell you, actually, the best bits – are corny. Cos truth is. Corny. I mustn't get hiccups. (*Swallows.*) Make love to me.

A pause.

MARK. No, I don't – no.

JUDITH. We've only tried once.

MARK. I'm just – not going through that again.

JUDITH. 'Going through'?

MARK. I can't, please –

JUDITH. You make sex sound like going through a shredder.

MARK. Well it is with you.

JUDITH. What do you mean?

MARK. You – scratch. You wriggle about.

JUDITH. Well –

MARK. Why couldn't you just –

JUDITH. What? Lie there?

This is very difficult for him.

MARK. Yes. Be the woman. Be obedient.

JUDITH. So you could what, come in peace?

MARK. I'm not getting into your crude talk, no –

JUDITH. What is it with you, this 'be the woman, be the man'?
Don't you like love-making? Oh. Am I the – oh, Mark –

MARK. This isn't working out. I want you to get your own place.

JUDITH. What?

MARK. I don't want you here. It's unseemly.

JUDITH. Why, who's looking? Don't tell me, God!

MARK. Go!

JUDITH. What, now?

A pause.

You want me to leave now?

A pause.

Go out into the city, now?

A pause.

In Rose Hill? The dangerous streets? Like this, with nothing
on?

A pause.

Cos I will if you want.

A pause.

I'll go. I'll disappear.

A pause.

Step backwards. So you won't see me. Ever have to think of
me again. Cos going into the night, it'd be like drowning.
And sometimes that's what I want, to step backwards, into
water, into the dark, disappear.

A pause.

You could wriggle about too.

A moment. Then he throws himself into her arms.

A blackout.

Lights up.

JUDITH *and* MARK *are asleep, she is sprawled across him, the 'bed' is even more disorderly. Her mobile phone is on the floor.* MARK*'s clothes lie where they were thrown off.*

A silence.

The mobile phone buzzes an email. Nothing from the sleepers.

Then JUDITH *wakes, feels around for the phone. Pulls it toward her. Fumbles to use it.*

MARK *wakes.*

MARK. What's happening, what's wrong, oh no –

JUDITH. Not sent, in! Inbox!

MARK. Get off me!

He recoils from her, she is fixated on the phone.

JUDITH. I asked the woman at Havant, she said she'd send
'em –

MARK *is pulling on his clothes.*

MARK. I didn't want to do this, why did I do this? I've got to
wash –

JUDITH. Yeah yeah!

One leg in his trousers, trying to get the other in, hopping.

MARK. We've got to talk, we've got to be serious, oh God,
help me, help me!

He falls over his trousers.

I never want to see you again, ever ever!

JUDITH. No, no, that's wrong, they're not my grades, that's wrong, no, oh shit! Shit!

She throws the phone across the stage and thumps the bed in a rage.

Scene Four

Christminster College. DEIDRE*'s rooms. She is on the phone. Someone is talking heated torrents at her.*

DEIDRE. No I'd be very, very chary of taking this to the Vice-Chancellor.

Listens.

Because we both know he's a one-man chamber of Chinese whispers. He'll misquote you. Deliberately. And anyway – I think it's a bad idea.

Listens.

Yes, I've seen the projected percentage of admission fees –

Cut off by the speaker. Listens.

But budgets are a form of propaganda, nothing to do with what actually gets spent –

She closes her eyes, very weary, she holds her face in her hand. The speaker goes on at some length.

You know there used to be a notion that a university's purpose is to encourage genius.

Listens.

No I said 'genius' not 'genetics' – (*To herself. Phone to her shoulder.*) help, help, they're taking over, someone help me! (*Back into the phone.*) Individual genius. Aren't we here to find great minds?

Listens.

I know you are trying to address the fee-paying deficit but if we lose sight of first principles –

Listens.

Well, Linda, if you want to call me that, do. Personally I think we need elites. I go into hospital, I want an elite surgeon – I get on a bus, I want an elite bus driver.

Listens.

Yes, yes, all right, going off-track here. Yes.

Sighs, listens.

Absolutely.

A beat.

Absolutely.

A beat.

Okay, a memo is a way to go – but keep it in-college, for now. Excellent, terrific.

A beat.

Bullet points. Bullet points are good.

A beat.

Absolutely. Yes.

She puts the phone down.

Jesus fucking Ada.

She pours herself a glass of whisky.

Enter JUDITH.

DEIDRE *turns and sees her.*

JUDITH. Hello.

DEIDRE. Hello.

DEIDRE *does not recognise her.*

You opened my door.

JUDITH. I knocked.

DEIDRE. I was on the phone.

JUDITH. My grades are wrong!

DEIDRE. I'm sorry –

JUDITH. They're not my grades! They got mixed up with someone else!

DEIDRE. Oh you're Sally Phillotson's little – Yes.

JUDITH *has not taken in the 'little'. Stamping her foot, a childish tantrum.*

JUDITH. The results are fake, fake, fake! It's fucking, fucking, fucking unfair! I've got to do it! For the people in the boat! For my father. Oxford he said, Oxford, get there, Jude! Do anything, just get there! Oxford, England! So I got to!

DEIDRE. Hey hey –

JUDITH. For him for the people in the boat for, for, for – got to, got to!

DEIDRE. Just calm down, girl, just –

JUDITH *staring at her.*

A pause.

Judith, isn't it?

JUDITH *stares at her.*

JUDITH. Do you really remember me?

DEIDRE. Of course I do. You're a cleaner, against all the odds trying to teach yourself Greek and Latin. How could I forget that – in this age of the spoonfed young whimpering in their safe spaces? Just tell me your grades.

JUDITH. A-star for Greek, A-star for Latin, but a stupid, stupid, wrong B-plus for Classical Civilisation.

DEIDRE *is stunned.*

DEIDRE. You got starred As for Greek and Latin languages?

JUDITH. But the B-plus for Classical Civilisation, that's got to be wrong!

DEIDRE. The language papers are the tough ones. Classical Civilisation is a nice little paper, but soft. Lesser gifted students take it along with Theatre Studies.

JUDITH. But I'm brilliant about classical times.

DEIDRE. Then you must have written something really stupid in an answer. Actually – I shouldn't let you know this but – I set one of the questions.

JUDITH. You mark the paper?

DEIDRE. No no, the marking's done by slaves in the outer provinces.

JUDITH. Then one of your slaves marked me wrong.

DEIDRE. There's a heavy-duty checking system. Exam boards live in fear of being sued by angry parents.

JUDITH. But my parents are dead!

A pause.

DEIDRE. You've done incredibly well. I'm sure those results are yours, I'll verify them – oh for Godsake, sit down.

JUDITH. I will if I can have one of those.

DEIDRE, *realising the glass is still in her hand.*

DEIDRE. Oh, this was a mistake –

JUDITH. Great mistake, though. Twisty word, great. Can mean bigly good or bigly bad.

DEIDRE. Bigly's not really an English adjective. As I think you well know –

JUDITH. Is now, I made it up!

DEIDRE *smiles*.

DEIDRE. Coin the language!

JUDITH. That's how you learn languages, in't it – you make 'em up for yourself, as you go along.

DEIDRE. You may. (*A beat.*) Oh – sod it. Sit!

She goes to pour them both a drink.

Your English is perfect. All but demotic – how long did it take you –

JUDITH. Oh, we learnt English in school in Syria.

DEIDRE. So, your family, I mean, your father was he in the –

JUDITH *looks at her, giving her nothing*.

Sorry I don't mean to –

As if JUDITH *has not heard that*.

JUDITH. Of course I didn't really get English till I got here.

DEIDRE. When you were –

JUDITH. I was eleven.

Moves on at once.

It's the twists and flicks in the way people speak. You can't get that from books and tapes. That's what makes you see what's being said, and that's what really matters in't it, not grammar and stuff. Language is speech that makes pictures in your head.

DEIDRE. Well – perhaps.

Handing JUDITH *a drink*.

Congratulations.

JUDITH. No. Commiserations. Cos I'm fucked.

DEIDRE. A common condition, my dear.

JUDITH. Tell me about it.

They both take a good sip.

DEIDRE. I wonder – what board did you sit? My question on
the Civilisation paper was about the gods in the *Iliad* –

JUDITH. Oh yeah! 'Discuss the reaction of Homer's heroes to
the power of the gods.' Did that one. And they don't.

DEIDRE. Don't –

JUDITH. React. Not like us. They're not awake, not conscious.

DEIDRE. Then how do they – do anything?

JUDITH. They do what the gods tell them to do. They actually
see the gods. And hear them. They don't think, they don't
decide. At a crisis, moment when they're really worked up –
battle, a row – a god appears and tells them what to do.
They've got no conscious minds like we say we have.
There's no thinking about themselves.

DEIDRE. No introspection. (*Considers for a moment.*) Well –

JUDITH. I've tried to imagine what it was like, but it's weird.
We've got this thing in our heads – just in front and around us,
a kind of space, yes? Where I know I'm me and you know
you're you. But they didn't have that. And when you look at
the language in the *Iliad*, there's no real word for mind.

DEIDRE. 'Psyche'?

JUDITH. 'Psyche' came to mean mind later. In the poem it
means body things, breath, blood – a dying warrior bleeds
out his 'psyche' into the dirt.

DEIDRE. What about 'thumos', soul?

JUDITH. But it don't mean what we call soul! Just – agitation,
movement. When a man stops moving, his 'thumos' leaves
his limbs. 'Psyche' and 'thumos', they're nothing like what
we call 'mind' or 'soul'. They're like organs in the body –
your kidneys, your liver. If you're a hero in the *Iliad*, they
work without you thinking at all. There isn't any thinking,
there isn't any 'will' in the poem, men are god-driven.
Athena appears, grabs Achilles by his hair, tells him not to

strike Agamemnon. The goddess Iris whispers to Helen and fills her with longing for her home. Paris doesn't decide to stop fighting, Aphrodite hides him in a mist on the battlefield and spirits him away. Athena appears as a Trojan and tells Hector to attack. It's the gods who start quarrels amongst men, send rumours through the camp – a god makes Achilles promise not to go into battle, another tells him to fight after all, another clothes him in fire and screams through his throat at the Trojans, driving them wild with fear. Actions have nothing to do with conscious plans, reasons – they are all in the actions and speeches of the gods. The gods take the place of consciousness. Except for one man. Who is beginning to be like us.

DEIDRE. Odysseus?

JUDITH. Odysseus. He's waking up. Full of wiles, as Homer says. Deceit. Cunning.

DEIDRE. And pain.

JUDITH. Yes. Cos he sets out for a homeland against the will of the gods.

DEIDRE. Like you did?

> JUDITH *stares at her, she will never reply to personal questions.*
>
> *A silence.*
>
> *Then* DEIDRE *moves to the drinks.*
>
> I need another drink.

JUDITH. Yes please.

DEIDRE. And that's what you wrote in your answer?

JUDITH. Yeah.

DEIDRE. Well, there's your smoking gun. That lost you your starred A.

JUDITH. Why?

DEIDRE. Jaynes.

Handing a drink to her.

Own up. You got that guff from Julian Jaynes.

JUDITH. Who?

She has not taken the drink.

DEIDRE. One of the great mad books, *The Origin of Consciousness in the Breakdown of the Bicameral Mind.*

JUDITH. You saying I nicked my answer?

DEIDRE. You're a very bright girl, you just used Jaynes's theories. The only trouble is, Jaynes is a red rag to academia. That's why you got marked down.

She is still holding the drink out.

JUDITH *glares at her.*

JUDITH. I've not read the fucking book! They're my ideas!

JUDITH *takes the glass and drinks it in one. She thrusts it back at* DEIDRE, *who takes it.*

A pause.

DEIDRE. My oh my. Why do I believe you?

JUDITH. Cos the goddess told you to.

They look at each other. Then they laugh.

DEIDRE. I'm giving you a place.

JUDITH. Place?

DEIDRE. There's a Classics faculty scholarship. I'm going to make sure you get it.

JUDITH. Place?

DEIDRE. Yes.

JUDITH. You're letting me in.

DEIDRE. I'll have to do the Oxbridge behind-the-scenes thing, the pulling out of teeth, the pulling in of favours, but don't bother your pretty little head about that.

JUDITH. You're letting me in.

DEIDRE. With the scholarship the fees won't be a problem but you're going to need something to live on.

JUDITH. I can clean, at night.

DEIDRE. I'm sure there's a way to help.

JUDITH. I'm in to Oxford.

DEIDRE. The college will get on to the Home Office, straighten out any immigration nonsense.

JUDITH. I'm in.

She covers her face and begins to weep.

DEIDRE. Oh come on, Judith.

JUDITH *sinks to her knees shaking with sobs.*

I think another drink.

JUDITH *removes her hands. She looks up at* DEIDRE, *her face tear-stained.*

JUDITH. I must tell – I must tell – my father.

DEIDRE, *moving toward the drinks, stops.*

DEIDRE. But – didn't you say – he –

JUDITH. Tell him in the land of the dead.

Scene Five

Rose Hill flat.

JUDITH *is tidying up.*

Doorbell.

She exits then re-enters with SALLY.

Awkwardness.

SALLY. I heard the news about your scholarship.

JUDITH. Yeah?

SALLY. Congratulations.

JUDITH. Thanks.

    A pause.

SALLY. Judith, I –

JUDITH (*interrupting*). I'd offer you a drink but I poured my last vodka down the toilet yesterday.

SALLY. A sober undergraduate? Original in everything. I want to say –

JUDITH. Sorry. You want to say sorry.

SALLY. I abandoned you in Waterlooville.

JUDITH. It don't matter.

SALLY. I was selfish.

JUDITH. It don't matter.

SALLY. I was all 'career career' –

    JUDITH *laughs.*

JUDITH. Said I was going to do a Medea on you. Poisoned cloak.

SALLY. You did.

JUDITH. Okay, you say sorry for abandoning me, I'll say sorry for Medea-ring you.

SALLY. I –

JUDITH. Well. Here we are, on the shore, the blessed shore.
   We've both got in to fucking Oxford!

SALLY. Yes – so we have.

JUDITH. Well there you go.

They hesitate – embrace or not?

SALLY. Look, there's a – tricky thing, say no if you – but
   Deidre Cass wants me to be your tutor.

A pause.

JUDITH. Yeah. Great. You're a terrific teacher.

Another hesitation then they move to embrace.

Scene Six

Night.

DEIDRE *coming out of a house.*

A woman's voice, off.

VOICE. Goodnight, Deidre!

DEIDRE. Night, darling!

VOICE. You can still Uber?

DEIDRE. Walk back to college will do me good.

VOICE. Sure?

DEIDRE. Don't worry I'm absolutely tippy-toes.

VOICE. Love!

DEIDRE. Love!

She turns away.

Enter PAT *at a distance, in the dark, observing her.*

Ah yes, I did love her once. But that was in another era – and beside the wench is – not what she used to be.

She laughs and walks. And suddenly PAT *is in front of her.*

PAT. Deidre?

DEIDRE. What? Who –

PAT. It's Patricia. Patricia Nash.

DEIDRE. Oh, Patricia! Nearly made me pepper.

PAT. You do remember me?

DEIDRE. Don't be silly, how could I not? Darling –

They kiss cheeks.

You were the brightest and the best.

PAT. I suspect you say that to all your old students.

DEIDRE. Only the – pretty ones. Ooops, sorry, a little the worst.

PAT. Actually I could do with a drink. Fancy a nightcap?

DEIDRE. Sweet of you. But late-night Oxford is dead these days.

PAT. I'm staying at The Randolph. We can go there.

DEIDRE. Ah, temptation. But tomorrow's heavy and –

PAT. Please. There's something I must talk to you about.

DEIDRE. Must?

A pause.

What are you doing in Park Town?

PAT. You need help.

DEIDRE. Do I now. This isn't chance, is it. What, am I under surveillance? I got you your job, you know.

PAT. And I'm very happy in the DOT.

DEIDRE *laughs.*

DEIDRE. The Department of Transport, yes! In the noughties we were all under pressure to recommend bright young things. Put you forward as a bit of a piss-take. A Trotskyist spook, why not! Knocked me down with a feather when you accepted.

PAT (*low*). You stupid, vain old woman. I'm doing this as a friend. We will now walk arm in arm, rather merry, to The Randolph Hotel. And I will save your life.

A moment, they are still.

A blackout.

Scene Seven

DEIDRE*'s rooms at Christminster College.*

She is sitting in the dark, dead still.

Enter SALLY.

SALLY. For Godsake, the smell in here.

DEIDRE. It's me.

SALLY. Well at least you've opened the door.

DEIDRE. Oh. New booze delivery. Forgot to lock door.

SALLY. Right, light, air, I'll –

DEIDRE. No no! Don't take my fug away. Athena's mist.

SALLY. Really, Deidre –

DEIDRE. Just sit with me. Sit!

SALLY *sits.*

A pause.

I've been threatened.

SALLY. Who by?

A pause.

Deidre?

DEIDRE. Maybe there is no deep state. No one's in charge. We're all one single cell. One amoeba. Which just – reacts when prodded. My country is a mindless entity.

She laughs.

Just – musing. Tugging the tether. Seeing how long it is. How tight.

SALLY. What's brought this on –

DEIDRE. I said – I've been threatened.

SALLY. We told you, Deidre, don't Twitter! You're – a powerful woman, you – go on *Question Time* and are rude about men. And you have grey hair.

DEIDRE. No, I have fun with my Twitter trolls. I poke them. No, I've been threatened by the real thing. A real troll. A little demon, popped up from underground.

SALLY. Oh Deidre, it's not sex –

DEIDRE. If only it were! No, this is not the caress of a delectable young thigh, come back to haunt.

SALLY. So it's the police –

DEIDRE. Not really police.

They are looking at each other.

A pause.

Ah. You just felt it. A fear like no other. Chest tight, head scrambled into horrible images, handcuffs, light-bulb rooms.

SALLY. Don't say this is to do with Judith.

DEIDRE. This is to do with Judith.

SALLY *closes her eyes with a sigh.*

The cousin she lives with has become a 'Subject of Interest'. So I have been told that – giving her a scholarship to this college is 'not in the National Interest'.

SALLY. That is outrageous. This isn't a police state!

DEIDRE. I begin to think that depends on who you are.

SALLY. We'll get a lawyer. I'll ring – I know who. And we'll go public. Twitter, the *Guardian* –

DEIDRE. Actually the threat was kindly meant. Delivered by an ex-student who – never mind –

SALLY. We'll name them, expose them –

DEIDRE. I've done the deed. I've had the faculty withdraw the scholarship.

A pause.

SALLY. You can't do that to her.

DEIDRE. School for terrorists? Write your own *Daily Mail*. The scandal could destroy everything I've tried to do in this college.

SALLY. No way would – Judith's in to Classical Greece, Western culture, what you and I – what we're meant to stand for!

DEIDRE. But – my source, my nemesis – tells me her cousin, this Mark, has gone Jihadist. I have to protect us from any taint. Or perception of taint.

SALLY. I can't believe you've done this.

A telephone rings. SALLY, *about to stand and answer.*

DEIDRE. Don't, it'll be her.

SALLY. How do you know?

DEIDRE. She'll have got the letter this morning.

They listen to the phone ringing.

SALLY. I'll answer!

DEIDRE. There are other clever girls, with starred A levels.

SALLY. And British passports?

The phone rings on, they listen. Then SALLY *breaks.*

It could be anyone, I –

She makes for the telephone. Just as she is about to lift it, the ringing stops.

DEIDRE. The walls are closing in. The space for what we believe, it's narrower and narrower. They can slam the walls together, crush us to death. And all the lovely things with it.

SALLY. What price, the lovely things?

The telephone rings again. SALLY *lifts it at once.*

(*Into the phone.*) Oh right.

Listens.

(*To* DEIDRE.) She's at the Porter's Lodge. They say you told them not to let her in. I think there's a bit of a scene, shall I –

DEIDRE. No. No.

SALLY *hesitates. Then into the phone.*

SALLY. I'm coming down.

Slams the phone down.

DEIDRE. We tell ourselves we're free. Transgressive. Making a new world. But, in the end, we are all collaborators.

SALLY *stares at her then rushes out.*

Scene Eight

Outside Christminster College.

A furious JUDITH *leaving. She has a screwed-up letter in her hand.*

SALLY *enters.*

SALLY. Judith, stop!

JUDITH. Stop, stop, yeah why don't I do that, stop!

SALLY. You know this is about Mark.

JUDITH. What you mean, 'about Mark'?

Realisation.

You mean – they sent me this –

Waves the letter.

– cos – That's shit!

SALLY. Judith –

JUDITH. Absolutely crapola lies and rubbish! Mark's always been moony about religion. When he was thirteen he was the only scientologist in Syria, till his father burnt his Ron Hubbards. Now he's got a touch of Islam but it's like the flu, he'll get over it, move on to Buddhism or – flat-earthing. He drives me mental, but I love him and – he's harmless.

SALLY. The police don't think so.

JUDITH. The college have told the police?

SALLY. No, the police told the college! Look, go to them. Volunteer a statement.

JUDITH. That's like saying volunteer to have your nipples ripped out.

SALLY. Police in England don't –

Stops herself.

JUDITH. Don't do that kind of thing? No? No? Cos they're Englishy not Araby, not foreigny, and will be so kindly, give me a cup of tea and say it's all right, dearie, dearie?

SALLY. Judith, you can do great things, I want to help you do great things, but you can't be –

Hesitates.

JUDITH. Can't be what?

SALLY. Extreme.

JUDITH. Extreme is good, extreme is pure, extreme is true, extreme is – clean!

SALLY. Maybe in Euripides, but not in life! Tell them all you know about Mark. Distance yourself. God forgive me – shop him!

A pause.

JUDITH. I can't believe you said that.

SALLY. Go to the police. Then Deidre and I can get the college –

JUDITH. Mark is family, know what that's meant to mean? No you can't, you're Western. In Syria, family's the house that's been bombed, the people that have been killed, cos when you're out on the roads in a foreign country, family is all that is left. You and that old woman with the whisky – you let me peep at heaven then you slammed the door. I'll never forgive her, I'll never forgive you.

Ζεύς σε γεννήτωρ ἐμὸς
πρόρριζον ἐκτρίψειεν οὐτάσας

She runs and exits.

SALLY (*translates*). 'Zeus, the father of my father's line,
Will blot you out utterly, raze you from the world.'

A pause.

What have I done?

Scene Nine

ROGER *and* PAT *are looking at* MARK, *who sits at a metal table, one wrist handcuffed. He has a polystyrene cup of water before him.*

Nothing for a while.

ROGER. It was you, wasn't it.

PAT. It was me what?

ROGER. Tipped off the lezzy professor.

> PAT s*tares at him.*

> Come on, Pat! It was a choice bit of Oldie Oxbridge Freemasonry. Did you sleep with her?

> *Nothing from her.*

> Whoa! When you were an undergraduate?

> *Nothing from her.*

> Mark the prof's card with that one.

PAT. Sorry if it's a bit overblown for you, Roger, but Deidre Cass is a great scholar and a wonderful teacher. She stands for true education. Free expression. Values we are here to protect, no?

ROGER. Not really. These days we're just rat-catchers.

> *She is about to protest.*

> Wait!

> *They look at* MARK *in anticipation.*

> Not yet.

> *A pause.*

> Don't worry, I didn't report you. Pain in the bum though, Judith the little genius doing a runner. Be hard to find.

PAT. The plod will pick her up.

ROGER. Don't bet on it, the country's arse-to-tail with CCTV but there are still dark corners. Get anywhere with Sally what's-her-name?

PAT. Scared well. But she's no idea where Judith is. What about the pig man?

ROGER. Says he hates the mother of his child but – y'know – secrets of the heart are a bugger.

A glance at him.

PAT. Indeed.

MARK *moves his free hand.*

ROGER. Oh!

They watch as MARK *puts out his free hand toward the polystyrene cup. His hand begins to shake but he manages to pick up the cup, moves it towards his lips but drops it, the water spilling over the table. He covers his head with his arm, sobbing.*

He's cooked.

PAT. Spilling the cup, always the sign they've broken. Sometimes I think we're just automatons. I'd better get in there, before, you know, in his trousers –

ROGER. No.

PAT. You want to interview him?

ROGER. There won't be an interview.

PAT. What do you mean?

ROGER. A new 451's on its way down from the mountaintop. We're prioritising – we've got to chase more Nazis.

PAT. The Nasrani cousins are no longer SOIs?

ROGER. He's Cat C now.

PAT. So we're letting him go?

ROGER. Oh we'll detain him the full twenty-eight days. Give him a bit of a lift.

PAT. And Judith?

ROGER. One more illegal. We'll pop her any time.

PAT. So much for πάντα κινῆσαι πέτρον.

ROGER. What?

PAT. Euripides tag. 'Leave no stone unturned.'

ROGER. Very helpful. Drink? Morpeth Arms?

PAT. Inevitably.

They link arms and begin to wander away, slowly.

ROGER. But, Miss Highly Educated Liberal State, from one angle – morally, morally –

PAT. God, Roger, that word in your mouth is sort of horrible –

ROGER. No, *morally*, you ruined the prospects of a brilliant individual, to protect an elite institution. How you feel about that?

PAT. Too many angles.

ROGER. Yeah. Rats in the maze are enough.

PAT. The girl was gifted.

He stops.

ROGER. Don't! Don't do that! I know you, Patricia Nash. You go maudlin, then you go guilty.

She takes his arm and they walk on.

PAT. Don't worry, all the guilt is squeezed away. Let's get pissed.

They exit.

MARK *is quietly sobbing at the metal table, his head hidden.*

A pause.

Scene Ten

JACK*'s farm.*

It is sunny and hot.

JUDITH *sits on the ground, sunk into herself. A stick lies before her. She has a padlock key in her hand. She is dead still.*

EURIPIDES *sits a distance away at the back.*

EURIPIDES. What has this country
                 Done to you?
  Filed your life down
  Till it is a life no more.

JUDITH. Oh shut up.

EURIPIDES. You are the swimmer that falls into a great sea.
  You cannot cross the towering wave above you.

JUDITH. Shut up!

  EURIPIDES *laughs.* JUDITH *picks up the stick and draws the Greek letters in the dirt. in the dirt.*

  Alpha. Omega.

EURIPIDES. Beginning
              To end.

  EURIPIDES *laughs again.*

  Enter MARTHA.

MARTHA. I know I'm not welcome. But I've come over anyway.

  A pause. She looks around.

  You're letting the garden die. The dahlias are drooping.

JUDITH. I like 'em droopy.

MARTHA. You want parched earth? Have parched earth.
  Where's Timmy?

JUDITH. Asleep.

MARTHA. I thought that child never slept.

JUDITH. It's the heat.

A pause.

MARTHA. Well? Has Jack phoned?

JUDITH *shakes her head.*

I thought you'd be there with him. On a day like this.

JUDITH. S'just another day.

MARTHA. He could lose everything!

JUDITH. You're going to go on, aren't you.

MARTHA. He's the father of your child!

JUDITH. 'Marry him.'

MARTHA. Marry him.

JUDITH. Even if he ends up in jail?

MARTHA. Prison's nothing in this country. Men come out.

JUDITH. On and on –

MARTHA. Do what's right.

JUDITH. Right. (*Chant.*) 'N' wrong 'n' right 'n' wrong right 'n' round 'n' round 'n' round –

MARTHA. I know he's a dog but we'll – train him. Put a collar on him. Have him sitting up nicely.

JUDITH. That what you want for me? A husband in a kennel in the yard?

MARTHA. What I want for you is a real life, not some – fantasy in your head. Be a British housewife with a British passport!

JUDITH. I'd rather put needles in my eyes.

MARTHA *closes her eyes, controlling herself.* JUDITH *continues to concentrate on drawing with the stick.*

MARTHA. The immigration, they can come for you, today, now. They'll be at that gate – big black car, big men, some stony-faced woman to take Timmy. They'll throw you in one of those centres, then God help you. Judith, you're back with your son now, be a family is the last hope.

JUDITH. Or – the last horror.

MARTHA. Sometimes the things you say – like you've got a fever on the brain! It's taken me sleepless nights, but – Jack the dog has a big heart. Letting Mark stay in the lower cottage. Not many men would be so generous – after what you got up to. Disgusting, two cousins!

JUDITH. You mean the Jihadism and the fucking?

MARTHA strides to her and slaps her face.

MARTHA. You stupid, foul-mouthed, nose-stuck-in-the-air, clever, clever, lump! Marry. Be safe.

JUDITH. Nowhere is safe, Auntie.

They stare at each other.

MARTHA. I don't care what you say, I'm going to hose –

Enter MARK. He now walks round-shouldered.

MARK. Mum, I'm going to witness.

MARTHA. You stay away from the court case or anything to do with it –

JUDITH goes back to drawing with her stick.

JUDITH. He doesn't mean law, he means religion.

MARK. I've got my pulpit in the barn –

He exits.

MARTHA. What did you do to my son?

JUDITH. I loved him.

MARTHA. Loved? You ruined him.

JUDITH. He's got the Nasrani nutter gene, that's all. I've got it, Timmy's got it. My father had it, walking across Europe, ranting about his little girl going to Oxford University? The Nasrani – thing. You just live with it.

She stops, staring at the point of her stick.

Or not.

MARTHA. No, it's you. Mark was a good boy, he had a nice little job, then you got your claws into him.

Enter MARK, *struggling with a street-preaching rig. A sign above his head is strapped onto his shoulders and waist, it reads: 'Back To Jesus'. He has a battery-operated amplifier slung rounds his neck and holds a microphone.*

MARK. Will you hear my witness?

MARTHA. Your what?

MARK. I've come back to Jesus.

MARTHA (*to* JUDITH). What have you put in his head now?

JUDITH. I'll hear it.

MARK. Great.

He turns on the microphone. There are squeaks.

Testing, Jesus is my saviour, testing, testing.

MARTHA *sinks to her knees.*

MARTHA. Mark, my dear, my sweet child.

MARK *sets himself. Then launches into –*

MARK. There are two cities in the world. Jerusalem and Babylon. The path to Babylon is wide. Along its way there are sellers of many delights, false gods tempting you into temples of sin, bodily sin, sin in your head. But the road to Jerusalem is narrow. Stony. Potholes and brambles along the way. Tears and cuts to the flesh. I wandered from the narrow path to the broad. But life is a journey. Lord Jesus called me back to the true way. Come, hold hands with Him, together we will go up to Jerusalem.

He turns off the microphone.

A silence.

His confidence has evaporated.

I thought – do it outside Fratton Park. When Pompey are playing. Bring the match-day crowd to Jesus.

MARTHA, *rising from her knees.*

MARTHA. Better preach to the pigs on this farm! Get all that off you! Now!

She flies at him, pulling at the rig.

Get it off! All of it! Now!

MARK. It's my pulpit –

MARTHA. Get it off!

MARK. Ow!

She pulls at him, they struggle. The rig is scattered. They both end up sitting on the ground, breathless.

JUDITH, *looking down at her stick.*

JUDITH. We're not on a journey. It's an illusion. We go nowhere. We are dead still.

MARK. No no, we're going to Jerusalem with Jesus, please –

He is very distressed. MARTHA *holds him.*

MARTHA. It's all right. You're coming home with me.

MARK. No no no no I'm here, with Jude –

JUDITH. Go with her. There's nothing for you here any more.

MARTHA *and* MARK *stand,* MARTHA *holding him.*

Say it to me, Auntie dear.

MARTHA. I think you're evil. I think you're a witch.

JUDITH. If only. Then I could magic a new land.

MARTHA. You have my curse. May you burn in fire.

JUDITH. Yes.

MARTHA *and* MARK *exit.*

EURIPIDES. In this age of the fake
                    The throwaway emotion
So bracing to feel
                    The power of a family curse.

JUDITH *is unmoved.*

EURIPIDES *stands, walks to* JUDITH *and sits beside her.*

You think you've suffered the worst thing in the world
                    But beyond
There's something more intolerable –
                    Everyday life.

JUDITH. Colour the dark more darkly. Love it, don't you.

EURIPIDES. I do my best.

JUDITH. Is it just a professional matter for you, tragedy?

EURIPIDES. Poets are only echoes.

JUDITH. Why did you leave Athens and go and hide in a cave?

EURIPIDES. I was trying to write my own story.

JUDITH. You mean it was a publicity stunt?

EURIPIDES. I was angry I'd just got second prize – again.
We're all human.

JUDITH. Thanks, poet, that really helps.

EURIPIDES. My pleasure.

Enter JACK. *He is sweating in a fine suit, his tie awry. He
carries a vodka bottle and has been drinking. He turns away
for a moment, arguing with himself, takes a swig, as –*

Here comes your Orestes
                    Your would-be rescuer.

JUDITH. Don't leave me. He'll talk about pork.

Having screwed up his courage, JACK *approaches* JUDITH.

JACK. I'm so sorry. Jude, I done my best, I really have, oh I so
wanted – everything – nice. For you, me, Tim. Poor fucking
loony Mark. And we were doing well, weren't we, for a bit!
On our way, weren't we! We had the Jeep Wrangler! And the
bikes. First. But now, look, even the dahlias haven't made it.
Heatwave? Yeah! Lovely weather for a fucking bankruptcy!
Cos that's what it is! Bank-bloody-rupted! But it's not my
fault! It's not! It's the fucking American free-trade pork! They
ought never have signed that deal! Free trade, free death.

He is breathless. He takes a swig from the bottle.

JUDITH *does not react.*

Well thanks for the love and tendering. Bit. Of. You don't
bloody help. You in't even drinking! Don't share a bottle let
alone a bed no more, I mean what happened to us? The great
times. Back in. Back. When the country. Yeah. Before. Now.

Breathless again. He goes to take another swig but does not.

But look we can be okay, we can. Climb back, Brit spirit.
Fuck 'em on the beaches. Entrepren – or. Ill. There's some
people in Pompey. They're a bit – y'know – but they'll help
me out with the fine. I can hang on to this place, though it
won't be pigs no more. Be – sort of transit stuff. (*A beat.*)
And we'll make you a Brit. Straight over to Havant, like
now! Registry office! Why not do it now? Smash the
immigration crap. Then begin again.

A pause.

JUDITH. Jerusalems and Babylons. Chewy Jerusalems, babbly
Babylons.

JACK. What?

JUDITH. I'm going to university.

JACK. Oh now, I thought we'd got rid of all that uni crap.

He struggles with himself. Then turns to her.

Jude, my love, Oxford, that's gone. Dead. Buried. For fucksake – they nearly did Mark for terrorism!

JUDITH. He's an innocent.

JACK. Yeah he's a sweet loony with an MI5 file!

EURIPIDES. To bear witness to all horrors.

JUDITH. He was bearing witness. To the sweet nutter that he is. That's all.

JACK. You're – tainted. Tainted meat. Oxford? The la-di-das won't come near you. Cos of Mark, cos of – it's horrible, but cos of what you are.

EURIPIDES. Tainted.

JUDITH. Tainted.

EURIPIDES. Hated foreigner.

JUDITH. Then that's what I'll be. The hated foreigner.

EURIPIDES. In a hated foreign land.

JUDITH. In a hated foreign land. Tainted. Like Medea.

JACK. Oh, the Greek shit, here it comes. Queen Media, that horrible play you wrote.

JUDITH. Translated.

EURIPIDES. My words in other tongues
                    Oh the horror –

JUDITH (*to* EURIPIDES). I did a fucking good job!

JACK. It were terrible. She killed her kids. Getting me to read it with you? God. You want to be her, don't you. You really do. In your twisted little mind, you think I'm what's-'is-name in the play? I mean how far you going to go?

JUDITH. All the way to university.

JACK. You –

JUDITH. Not Oxford. I'm going to start my own.

JACK. You –

JUDITH. I'll leave. Disappear. Over the border. I'm sorry, Jack.

JACK. You've – not done something. (*Terrible thought*.) Christ,
Timmy.

Calling out.

Timmy! Timmy!

He exits.

EURIPIDES *folds his cloak around* JUDITH.

The light is going as they disappear.

EURIPIDES. Zeus in Olympus

JUDITH. Zeus in Olympus

EURIPIDES. Sees everything we do

JUDITH. What the gods can achieve

EURIPIDES. What the gods can achieve
                    Is beyond our understanding

JUDITH. Guide me on my way
Artemis my sister

EURIPIDES. Send smooth seas, oh Goddess
                    For the unending journey

Of the beloved stranger.

They have disappeared. A pause and JACK *bounds back
onto the stage.*

JACK. He's fine! He wants his tea, and he wants a story, just
don't make it Greek for once, right? I'm sorry, Jude, I don't
know what I thought there for a moment – Jude? Jude? Jude?

End of play.